UNVEILED by TRUTH

THE WORD OF GOD

Jackie Moody

ISBN 979-8-88943-687-4 (paperback)
ISBN 979-8-88943-688-1 (digital)

Christian Faith Publishing
832 Park Avenue
Meadville, PA 16335
www.christianfaithpublishing.com

Printed in the United States of America

A Day with Death

One day, not if, but when death calls for you.
It'll be a bit late for blaming games, saying, "Only if I knew."

We all have an appointed day designed by death.
The chance is now, not when we take our last breath.

Life is just a vapor, it appears then vanishes away.
God gives us opportunity; it's up to us if we decide to stray.

Jesus loves us, and he'll never let us go.
His offer is free will. It's our choice if we say no.

A day with death is coming for you and me.
We'll then find out where we'll spend eternity.

Death is real, and there's no second chance.
There's no one on earth that can pray us through in advance.

It's available for anyone to have a one-on-one relationship with the
    Lord.
Jesus welcomes us with open arms, giving us a chance to get onboard.

A Liar

If you tell one lie, you'd have to tell two.
To cover up the first one, and hope no one knew.

Lies that are told are a danger to us all.
Pretty soon, you start believing them, and that's when you fall.

It's hard to remember all the lies you've told.
So, you make up another one, and hope it's sold.

The lies will pile up until no one would trust you.
Word is your bond, which could cause someone to sew.

Friendship destroyed, because they don't know what to believe.
True character is something that you must achieve.

The Bible says, "He that tell lies shall not tarry in his sight."
We can't even stand before a Holy God unless we do what is right.

Our lies separate us from having true love in our life.
It could break up a relationship between husband and a wife.

Lies could convict us and place us in jail.
Turn around, lose our life, then end up in hell.

Caused contracts on our life to have one killed.
Because the lies we told had soon been revealed.

Angry with God

I engaged in a conversation with someone I didn't know.
He started telling me about a loved one's death a long time ago.

It happened to be that this person was very close to him.
I found out it was his beautiful wife, who was once named Kim.

She died in a horrific accident, not too very long ago.
This darkened his heart, angry with God, while at a mere low.

Why didn't he save her, it wasn't hard for him to do?
He was the one to look to, in desperate times of going through.

I became angry with God, and gave up on life.
Bitter and resentment now turned quickly into strife.

How could he have let my dear loved one die.
Isn't he the Savior that watches over us from the sky?

I'm angry with God, because I thought he refused to hear.
That my wife was everything to me, I wanted her to always be near.

I asked why he ignored my cry, I felt small, "You were my only call."
He said he loves me, not to give up, he's with me throughout it all.

I'm a Father to her as well as you, she was prepared; I thought you knew.
I spoke to her in the middle of the night, her reply was, "He'll be alright."

I'm so sorry it painfully hurt you to take her life so soon.
My time may be followed by morning, night, or even sometimes noon.

I leave with you the comfort of my love, by my strength from thereof.
I'll continue to watch over you, draw you close and carry you through.

Anxiety

Anxiety is a robber and a thief; it steals your desire
    to increase.
It aggravates your mind, and thoughts, while sepa-
    rating true peace.

It robs you of your goals, and ambitions, then leads
    you to depression.
While listening to the enemy, he began conducting
    his evil sessions.

Symptoms include shortness of breath, imminent
    doom, and even death.
Overwhelming, intense fear, peaks within seconds,
    then cause bad health.

God is not the author of confusion, our enemy
    sends strong illusions.
Worrying seems to be a true fact for opening you up
    for a heart attack.

Feeling discomfort, like you're choking or not get-
    ting enough air.
Anxiety could also be the cause of you losing your
    hair.

These are just some of the things that we really need
    to let go.
Pray and meditate on the Word of God, and he will
    fix it, as so.

We live by faith, and not by sight; tell yourselves it's
     going to be alright.
Declare deliverance, all through life, this one's over,
     tomorrow's another fight.

Anxiety is an emotional response brought on by
     feelings and tension.
Often combined by worrying, and physical change,
     if I haven't mentioned.

There are good and bad anxieties, they're not all the
     same.
As when the birth of your first baby, or you forgot
     your boss's name.

Never let anxiety enter your hearts. Never worry
     about any of your needs.
The Lord is in control of our emotions, if we only
     stop and let him lead.

Appointment

Earthquakes, fire, drought, and heavy rain.
Mudslides, COVID-19; immediately wondering, "Who's to blame?"

Husbands killing wives, children committing suicide.
Families forced out of home, even though they've tried.

Heatstroke's on a high, hottest on record mankind's ever known.
Parents having nervous breakdowns, fear of having to leave their kids
    alone.

Hospitals in danger of collapse, due to people not wanting to adapt.
Killer hornets on the rise, last days are here, hey, no need to be
    surprised.

We all have an appointment, a day with death we can't break.
But good news, God will forgive us of all wrongs and mistakes.

Father God, in Jesus's precious name, we come with a sorrowful
    heart, full of pain.
Asking for forgiveness of all our sins, you alone we need to defend.

Cover us all, Lord, from these deadly attacks, and please put this
    nation back intact.
We can't do this, Father, without you, so we bow our heart and bend
    our knees asking that you help us please.

* * * * *

To God be the glory.
Thank you.

Be Careful Who You Let into Your Spirit

Be careful who you let into your spirit; everyone
    does not wish you well.
In fact, there are those that attach themselves to you
    while hoping you fail.

Proverbs tells us to guard our heart, because every-
    thing we do flows from it.
The enemy attaches himself to people in order for
    us to feel we're unfit.

He seeks for those who are vulnerable and insecure
    in their walk.
And overwhelms us with problems, until we just
    don't desire to talk.

To my God, that could help us through all that
    we're going through.
By reading and declaring through faith, there's noth-
    ing my God can't do.

He allows us to discern the Spirit that is trying to
    befriend us.
By exposing the person, and softly whispering, to
    our defense, "Don't trust!"

We override what he says and do what we want to
    do "our way."
Trying to please by not worrying what people would
    say.

We go through our life without ever trying to guard
    the spirit.
As we open ourselves up to be attacked while deny-
    ing the way we hear it.

What we really should be careful about when we're
    not standing near.
Is that the one we let in is whispering about us for
    others to hear.

When we're praying to our Father from up above.
Let's ask him to send us someone with true love.

Bullying

My mother told me to talk to her, my father, or
　　even a friend.
Being picked on in school, by bullying, while I'm
　　not able to defend.

I know she means well, but don't understand all I go
　　through.
I opened up to her, she told the staff, made things
　　worse, "Who knew."

Learning to keep to myself, no eye contact, just
　　glimpse and walk away.
You see, I couldn't go through another beatdown
　　this very same day.

I feel out of place because no one wants me around.
So, I sit quietly, eat fast, and hope I didn't make
　　much of a sound.

Which triggers a crew of kids that enjoys beating me
　　to the ground.
What have I done! Alone in my state of mind, with
　　no one to be found?

I suffer in silence, each day, tearing a piece of my
　　soul and my mind.
What should I do, I try to hide, the pain grew
　　worse; so left behind?

How could I escape, my attendance is required each
　　and every day?
In the midst of these hurtful classmates that have
　　nothing good to say.

I wish the principal, and staff, could see the hurt
    embedded in my soul.
To understand my pain and see my heart, enlarged
    with a big hole.

Once happy, and excited, to be there, but stress
    caused my loss of hair.
Which became another matter, eating disorder, as
    I've got fatter.

When you pick and hurt people, I need you to
    understand.
Our differences are to unite us, for that was always
    the Lord's plan.

Christmas

We celebrate your birth, Lord, on this very special day.
Nothing by far could compare where baby Jesus lay.

Your birth is so special, the angels gathered to see.
This historic dedication, prepared just for you and me.

Your birth changed our life, and it gave us hope.
The direction we're going will help us to cope.

You looked down from heaven and saw mankind lost.
The ultimate sacrifice, unfortunately, came with a cost.

We celebrate your birth on this beautiful Christmas Day.
A true miracle through Mary, what more could we say.

Your birth rendered you, as being, Lord and Savior.
Your purpose is simple, to change our behavior.

You're the perfect gift on this Christmas Day.
The son of God born, just to pave the way.

Cervical Sprain

I went to bed early one hot Friday night.
Anticipate on waking up on morning's first light.

Excited about working the food ministry at the church.
My mission was to do giveaways to all that is in search.

It didn't happen as planned as my morning unfold.
Tremendous pain ran down my neck, unable to be consoled.

This sprain was so severe, with spasms running down my neck.
Couldn't lift my head for one minute, my whole body was in a wreck.

I went to the hospital next day, early Sunday morning,
Fell to the floor with a scream, as the doctor began exploring.

She ran tests, took blood, and did a scan of my neck and back.
I was diagnosed with a cervical sprain injury, which caused the attack.

My doctor gave me about six weeks to heal properly, which was severe.
I prayed, because I needed help; by God's grace, I need him to appear.

The pain did subside; instead of six weeks, it took about four.
I credit it all to my Lord and Savior, who I wonderfully adore.

When I think of this severe cervical sprain that affected my neck.
I remember, desperately praying, as God had changed the side effects.

Deal with Your Situation

Throughout life, we have to learn to deal with
    situations.
Whatever direction we may go could cause extreme
    aggravation.

As a volcano when it begins to erupt, spew lava and
    fire, which can't be stopped.
Boiling water is another, often overflows because we
    refuse to step on toes.

Nothing good will come out of anything that is not
    rightfully dealt with.
Letting it go, and it will soon resolve itself; well,
    that's just a myth.

We allow what we will until it's too late, turn
    around and say, "This was my fate."
Then dare not to discuss, in fear it may just turn
    into a debate.

So, what do we accomplish when we lay silent in wait?
Anger builds up which will eventually turn into hate.

We deal with the matter even if we argue through-
    out the night.
That's better than holding everything in, never dis-
    cussing what wasn't right.

Deal with our situation, or it will surely deal with us.
Write it on paper, put a stamp on your letter, if you
    must.

This will help out for all involved and will allow us
    to be set free.
Then we wouldn't harbor any illness in our heart, by
    forgiving, and letting it be.

Covet

The tenth commandment in the Bible says "Thou
    shall not covet."
Thy neighbor's wife, house, manservant, ox, or ass—
    no one is above it.

The sin of coveting begins in our heart; desiring
    one's life is wrong from the start.
Jesus made clear in the Sermon on the Mount, "Do
    not covet, this sin tears apart."

Such as when Ahab did with Naboth's vineyard and
    David coveted Bathsheba.
While Ahab was greedy, David, touched by her beauty,
    killed for this diva.

When we covet, we give in to a toxic, selfish mind-
    set that leads to sin and death.
Wanting someone's else life, husband, wife, home,
    children, and even health.

The desire becomes so strong, until you defy all
    odds to accomplish your goal.
This is not a compliment; this was something
    unfolded, because you were bold.

The word is clear, the order is divine, the law is
    mandated for all times.
What God gave me is not for you; his grace and
    mercy will carry you through.

The tenth commandment says "Thou shall not covet."
Because having someone else's life, you may find,
    you really don't love it.

Death

We all have an appointment with death, regardless
    of our status or our wealth.
Not enough money, prestige, fame, or will can
    change this appointed deal.

The appointment has a judgment in sight; being
    good does not make you right.
Nor the ability to give everything away, we're still
    required to stand that day.

Death has no favorite, don't discriminate, take who
    it wants, that's its fate.
Immediately following, after the call, we will stand
    before God, who reveals it all.

Whether you're a pastor, member, or attendee, none
    will be able to flee.
Not being true, and real with our walk, the book
    will be open, for the Lord to talk.

What will he find when he calls for us, is it some-
    thing we'd hope he kept hush?
Death is final, there's no way back, heaven or hell;
    and that's just a fact.

Where will you spend eternity? Once you're sen-
	tenced, there's no escaping thee.
While we're alive, we still have a chance, it's not too
	late for our deliverance.

The thing about death—we don't know the hour or
	day, God has the final say.
Don't let it be said that it's too late, now is the time,
	for God will not wait.

Death of a Sister

I mourned the death of my sister for a very long
    time.
Depression set in; my behavior was a total mere
    sign.

It was so hard to keep a real smile on my face.
As long as I pretend and not show any real trace.

We were close, two years apart, best friends at most.
I remember, one Sunday afternoon, got the call, way
    too soon.

I had just come home from washing a load of
    clothes.
Saw a light blinking on my machine, listened, as it
    threw big blows.

Message left, Tracey was dead, couldn't comprehend
    what was said.
I walked around in a daze for years, going through
    the flow, fighting back tears.

Didn't once visit her at the grave, I didn't have
    enough strength to be brave.

If you could hear me, Tracey, I would like for you to
    know.
I still miss you, sis, I miss you so, even though it's
    been a long time ago.

One day I will see you, one day when I die, we'll
    rejoice with Jesus in the sky.

Twenty-eight years ago, just seems as it was not that
    long.
Because the memories that I have gave me a new
    song.

You're still my best friend, even though you're not
    here with me.
That will never go away, sweet memories, I have, if
    only you could see.

Disappearance: The Rapture

I woke up one morning, following my routine, as
    I've done each day.
This time was different, before I turned on the TV, I
    heard loud crying, as I lay.

Loud noises followed by, car tires screeching, sounds
    of accidents, dogs barking.
This was unusual, because the sound made it seem
    as if someone was out larking.

It was horrific in all that I've seen, much more
    chaos, remind me of a bad dream.
I've heard people are missing all over the nation,
Oh, what a scary conversation.

I was reminded of the words that were taught,
    preaching, "The rapture is near."
It meant nothing to me at that time, now it actually
    drives me into fear.

My body began to shake, during a series of calls, to
    whom I believed, served well.
These were those I looked up to, thinking they
    would not go to hell.

No answer, as fright crippled my body with fear, I
    realized the end was so near.
If only I'd believed what I've read in the Word, now
    it's too late, the time is here.

I prayed, and prayed, didn't know if it made a differ-
ence, so I ran to the church.
Waiting to see if anyone else had come, for one
purpose, and that was to search.

I did see some, who wasn't right; every Sunday, they
were engaged in a fight.
Then, to see them come to me, saying, that every-
thing was going to be alright.

If I could do it all over again, I would not sit on
Susie's row, and talk about Mike.
I closed my ear to the Word of God, thinking it's all
about me and who I like.

I was fooled by a lie, that the enemy whispered in
my ear, "You're young, have fun."
But what he didn't tell me was I took a chance of
missing the only begotten Son.

There is another way, and the only one that is avail-
able for me, and you.
Deny the mark of the beast, which the enemy has
not planned for us to do.

Fear

Fear is the opposite of faith.
Fear affects more than one-eighth.

Fear panics the heart to cringe.
Setting you on a path to binge.

Fear attacks your mind to worry.
Which leads you to act in a hurry.

Fear causes you to panic.
And opens a door through satanic.

Fear gives you a sense of anxiety.
Which is present throughout society.

Fear burns our heart with horror.
Through depression and sorrow.

Fear opens the door for sin.
Allowing the enemy to enter in.

Fear stops you from reaching your goal.
Binding pursuit, unless told.

Fear torments your very thought.
Changing everything you've been taught.

Fear emotionally causes you to tremble
Storing our feelings in a showcase as such type symbol.

Fear separates us from God.
To some, this may even seem odd.

Discernment

Father, I'm not asking for me to preach, neither do I desire to teach.
Not asking to sing in the choir, no, Lord, that's still not my desire.

Don't want to be a driver on the new church bus.
And listen to the saints, as they gather around and fuss.

No, not even being on the usher board, being unified and on one
accord.

But what I would desire, in the midst of it all.
Discerning of the spirit, to have an ear, for your call.

Not at all, that these duties in the church are bad.
For we must love the work that we do, rejoice in you, and be glad.

Discernment intersects the Christian life at every point.
As God reveals his knowledge in us, should be all that we ever want.

It is not optional for the believer, instead it is required.
But, not for those that simply wants to be admired.

Unfortunately, it is an area where most Christians stumble.
Unbiblical decision-making and bad behavior should make us
humble.

Failure to distinguish between truth and error.
Is subject to lead us to follow the mindset of one: Pharaoh.

Thessalonians teaches our responsibility to discern.
Examine everything carefully; hold fast to his Word, and learn.

Don't Flirt with the Devil

If you flirt with the devil, you will be in his bed.
That is an old saying, that was once said.

He doesn't care about you, nor does he care about me.
He fell from grace, determined for us "not to be free."

The Bible says he comes to steal, kill, and destroy.
Being allowed in our life is something we shouldn't enjoy.

He's the author of confusion and will tear our life apart.
His goal is to destroy us and shatter our dear heart.

If you flirt with the devil, he'll flirt back with you.
Remember, he's a deceiver, and his words are not true.

We must not allow him to be in control of our life.
For he is the wicked enemy that pours out strife.

He whispers in our ear just to fill our life with fear.
He wants our soul, but he's not the one in control.

His fate is sealed, and yes, he's running out of time.
When Jesus Christ appears, he will be chained in the pit for his crimes.

What God Allows

You allowed me to wake up, and see
another day; that's not promise to me.

You allowed food on my table, for my
family; dear Lord, I humbly praise thee.

You allowed me to retire from my job, as
you protected me from being robbed.

You allowed me to have a church home,
heavenly message from the throne.

You allowed me to have a wonderful husband
and beautiful kids—mine and his.

You allowed me to have the best parents and
in-laws, though their reputation is flawed.

You allowed us to have a beautiful and
warm home, where we're never alone.

You allowed us to have several vehicles,
to get around, this seems unfound.

You allowed us to have lots of sisters,
and brothers, and many others.

You allowed us to have clothes on our
back; with you, there is no lack.

You allowed us to have lots of accessories,
a bonus with sweet melodies.

What God allowed for you and
me, he allowed for all to see.

Health

Health is one of the most important things in life.
Many would give all, as well as going under the knife.

It helps us to evaluate our life, at its most.
By giving us a new perspective, throughout the coast.

We are to exercise, eat right, and take care of our body.
Splurge if we must, but not always be naughty.

Sleep is necessary, it gives our body the proper rest.
Then we're rejuvenated, and again at our best.

Our bodies are temples of the Holy Spirit.
For that purpose, we shouldn't want anything bad near it.

Water is also definitely good for our health.
Life depends on it, regardless of our wealth.

We pray over our medicine, and take it as well.
And ask God to work through it, so our body won't be frail.

Vitamins play an important role, help with nutrients, as I'm told.
Let's take care of our body, by keeping our health under control.

Heartbeat

God, I feel your heart beating through mine.
I don't know how to describe it, so I'll just say, "It's divine."

When I'm bitter, from hurt, and want to let it go.
The stronger beat, over-rhythms my heart, and lets me know.

Oh, how I truly love how you have pulled me along.
Your presence presides in me and gives me a brand-new song.

You've helped me along the way, and yes, it has been tough.
But with you, by my side, I could overcome all kind of stuff.

My heart beats in awe of you, as it waits for your touch.
Which to me, all that I've ever desired and hoped for so much.

You are so good to me, Lord, and I'll tell you the reason why.
Because there's no one on this earth that could have drawn me nigh.

My heart beats, in twine of you, and that's all I need to make it through.

Humility

Humility is a choice; it is something we
are required to do, on our own.

Humility is not thinking less of yourself; it's
thinking of yourself less, "as shown."

Humility is an act of the will; for some,
it just doesn't fit their appeal.

Humility is "the state of being humble," a
strong line between humility and grace.

Humility is freedom from pride or arrogance,
and keep you on a visible but solid face.

Humility is often characterized as genuine,
gratitude, and lack of arrogance.

Humility is low self, a liberation from
acceptance, as well as appearance.

Humility is critical and conscious, emphasis
of godliness concerning Christ.

Humility is an act, shown how Jesus went
to the cross, pierced, with sacrifice.

Humility is giving up the right to be labelled
as wrong; some call it strung along.

Humility is said, pride comes, then comes
disgrace, with humility comes wisdom.

Humility is also known as being simple,
seen as weak as would some.

Hurt People Hurt People

There's an old saying, "Hurt people
hurt people," which is true in itself.

They do what's been done to them, trying
to ease the scars that's been left.

Sometimes, as a child, when you've been
traumatic and repeatedly abused.

The pattern is followed by you, because
you are now simply confused.

Mistaking hurt for love, pain for fear,
attacking any and all who come near.

Hurt people hurt people, they
sometimes see no other way.

Let's pray for them, cover them,
and not throw them away.

Only God can heal the broken in heart,
and restore you to a new start.

We all have hurt that we harbor inside, on
our knees in prayer is how we abide.

Some of us have been so broken, a dose
of daily drugs is our only token.

We don't know how to fight, because no
one took the time to show the light.

So confused, and don't know where to go,
until Jesus, the Savior, lets you know.

He's the only begotten Son, who has the
power to change all that was done.

Husband

I fell in love with you, Steve, from the first day we met.
At that time, we weren't saved nor delivered as of yet.

Young lady, running from the Lord, trying to find my own way.
Not realizing it was all in his plan to change our life that day.

Soon after, we got married, and was very young in age.
It didn't stop us, we both were glowing, and on the same page.

Through repentance, Jesus changed our lives, all forevermore.
The sweetest day of our life—oh, how we both truly adore.

We struggled these thirty-three years, three children, and five grands.
But God, in his infinite wisdom, he would forever have a plan.

The good outweighs the bad in all we've ever gone through.
Family vacations, getting away, and traveling is what we knew.

We've done well, in our life together, forever, and to the end.
Are the vows we made unto God, my lover and my friend.

I Listened to the Enemy

I listened to the enemy as he spoke lies in my head.
He said, next week, this time, I would be dead.

He tried to influence me, to take my own life.
By arranging and rearranging for the purchase of a knife.

I was convinced I had no friends, I was on my own.
Not wanting me to remember God sits on the throne.

He continued to feed me lies as I listened to his game.
If only I was strong enough to remember to call on Jesus's name.

I went on this pity party for weeks at a time.
Thoughts came in my mind about committing a crime.

That's the enemy strategy: when low, up the blow.
Then act like he cares so that no one would know.

He can't love you; his assignment is for our fall once and for all.
But God has a plan; in the Master's hand, he will come to our call.

Jesus loves us, and he will forever be near.
Not by force, it's our choice, nor by fear.

His hands are stretched wide, he's on our side.
He knows your name; he'll take away your shame.

I'm Not Perfect

Look at me; I'm not perfect, but neither are you.
I've done awful things in my life, some, only God knew.

You've been with me, Lord, every step of the way.
Although my ultimate desire was to one day stray.

I didn't want to give up on things I wanted, nor what I controlled.
Had no desire to give you my life, in fear of my plans to unfold.

You loved me, and held me, even though I turned away.
By shielding, and protecting me, while prompting me to stay.

I came back to repent, thinking; what would I lose?
The enemy had me in a trance, hoping I had no need to choose.

No, I'm not perfect, and God is not requiring it to be so.
Just open your heart, humble yourself, and let him lead the show.

Who could find such a love, that could draw you near?
Forgive all of your sins, and wipe away your tears.

There's not a man on earth, only God above.
That could fill our hearts and mind with this kind of love.

In Between the Lines

All of us at some point have learned to read, in between the lines.
An instinct that God placed in us by allowing us to see the signs.

We've all had hidden agendas we want no one to learn about.
For the sake of being protected, we open our senses when in doubt.

You learn what is truth as you listen to spoken words.
In between the lines, we discover the true meaning, what we've heard.

If we're often silent, rather than noisy, and listen with our heart.
Hidden or implied meanings will not be very hard to see apart.

In the case of a job, when they're trying to find a way to let you go.
It's not what's being said, or even the smile in their face, "you know."

Or your teenage child that compliments you throughout the day.
You know deep down, they're up to something, but just won't say.

In between the lines is something we all should pay more attention
     to.
Then we wouldn't be caught off guard by not knowing what to do.

Jesus, You Know My Name

Jesus, you know my name, the only one with supernatural fame.
You called me when I was in my mom's womb, while waiting to be
  groomed.

You followed me, Jesus, throughout my entire life.
Watching and protecting me, from all hurt, harm, and strife.

You cradled me, from birth, up, and until now.
Through forgiveness, only you can allow.

Jesus, you are the one that knows my name.
Before I was thought of, through your power, I became.

My destiny, and my life, has already been planned.
For God alone, design is in the master's hand.

You know all of my faults, my desire, and my pain.
Throughout it all, your name, Lord, I will always proclaim.

When I was homeless, and living in the streets.
You sent your angels to protect me; now, no one will mistreat.

Jesus, you know my name, because I'm forever yours.
Through guidance, and deliverance, you showered with outpours.

Jesus Betrayed with a Kiss

Judas, how could you betray my Lord, with the
word "Rabbi!" and a kiss.
Did you not know he is Jehovah, and he would be
forever missed?

Condemned by thirty pieces of silver, by the chief
priest, and the thief.
He died on the cross, for you and me, for a debt we
owe, he paid for us to be free.

With him came a crowd armed with swords and
clubs, and evil men using scrubs.
Seized and arrested him, without even a fuss; divine
truly, allowed if they must.

What he didn't understand, was all of this written,
was a part of God's plan.
His death alone brought attention to all, so
humankind would get a fair hand.

How, Judas, you couldn't see, the Messiah, Jesus,
was real to thee.
You listen to the enemy within, all because of hatred
men.

This set the tone for all eternity, one day he'll be
back, just wait, y'all see.
His return will be without spot or wrinkle, in saving
someone like me.

Some won't believe, they say it's a lie, "what if you're
      wrong" and choose to deny.
You will lose all that you have, because you turned
      your back on him in the sky.

He was beaten without recognition; no man could
      have endured, just to mention.
This is not the end of the story; after three days, he
      rose again in glory.

That would be such a wonderful day, when the sky
      would crack and my Lord would say.
"Well done, thy good and faithful servants, your
      place is reserved for you this day."

Loving God

In the arms of a loving God is where all safety is found.
Our enemy, the adversary, is seeking whom he may turn around.
He doesn't care how it's done; his goal is to get back at the Son.
In the good times and the bad, it's God alone who sits on the throne.
He said he would never leave us, nor forsake us; we are never alone.
His ways are not ours, nor do we always understand what's going on.
You are my worship, Lord, and you are sincerely my praise.
I pray to you, for I don't know what may come in the near days.
We thank you, dear God, for your mercy and your grace.
One nation under God is what we will always and forever embrace.

Mama Rose

It's been years since you've gone home, but the
    memories, they won't fade.
I catch myself reminiscing on conversations, and the
    beauty you displayed.

I miss you, Mama Rose, that beautiful laughter and
    unforgettable smile.
You could pull out the best in any situation, which I
    haven't seen in a while.

Your heart, I miss, was as pure as gold—this I know,
    not what I was told.
I honor you in all that you've done, understanding
    that everything wasn't fun.

You let your light shine so that all of your family
    were able to see.
The goodness, of the glory of the Lord, shining
    brightly in thee.

You left your legacy, for your family to follow: God
    first—easy to swallow.
We visit your resting place, from time to time,
    knowing your flight was God's design.

I pray, you're looking down over us, to guide our
    hearts, when we're about to fuss.
I call you my angel, from up on high, you said to
    me; you know, and I do: you're in the sky.

Goodbye, farewell, my beautiful Mama Rose, you're
    the one our good Lord chose.
Your family will miss you forevermore, you are the
    example; oh, how they adore.

You made a difference in each of them, in your own
    way, reflecting your love day by day.
Your presence still presides there, in your home,
    telling us we're not alone.

Mental Illness

We must always pray for those that are in need.
We see the enemy, trying to come against the
      people, and their seed.

Through mental health, abuse, depression, and
      suicide.
People don't know where to go, who to talk to, or
      where to hide.

Husbands beating their wives, mothers killing their
      sons.
Depression speaking to your head, while suicide
      seems to be for fun.

Families are hungry, with no money or food in
      sight.
Hearts are failing, people are dying with no sense of
      wrong, or right.

There is a God, that understands and knows what's
      going on in our life.
In time, the Lord will deliver us from all hurt, harm,
      and strife.

Murders everywhere are going up, with increasingly
	tremendous highs.
To not allow someone in a store without a mask; we
	hear, some dies.

That's not the end of the story, murder hornet
	becomes another reason to worry.
For those of us in need of a savior, let's raise those
	hands, for all who are in favor.

I choose Jesus Christ, hands up: no shame, without
	a second thought.
He gets my commitment, and my vote, there's no
	way I'm willing to be bought.

Miraculous

God is the only one that causes miracles, he is
  miraculous on his own.
The true and rightful owner that has all rights to sit
  on a holy throne.

Any type of superhuman, or astounding event, all
  gives glory to God.
It shouldn't be unthinkable, unbelievable, or even
  suggested as odd.

When a plane crashed, and the only survivor is a
  baby, that's extraordinary.
Or making it out alive, after being involved in a
  head-on collision, by voluntary.

God is supreme, and above all that is, or has ever
  been heard of in history.
The fact that he is phenomenal, amazing, and
  sensational, "some say a mystery."

It's been known, and written about, the mind-
  blowing raising of the dead.
Only a divine, powerful, everlasting God could hold
  that title, "as some has said."

Whether you believe or not, we must admit, his
	name is mentioned through life.
God is the only one that causes miracles,
	miraculous, even in his advice.

I couldn't leave such a God like this, walking away is
	not something I want to risk.
Healing is miraculous in itself, sick one day, healing
	and cured, as I began to pray.

Every situation is different, yours may not come the
	way mine came.
The miracle he has for you may involve a whole
	different ball game.

Order

The ocean, and the sea, has its order.
Neither are they allowed to go beyond their border.

Unless, God allows through tsunami, wind, or
    storm.
That's the only way, through; shape or form.

The sun shines, and it gives the world its light.
The moon has boundaries, and gives lesser light, at
    night.

The climate, also has its orders, winter, spring,
    summer, and fall.
Which is determined, by the weather's climate,
    throughout it all.

The stars, give light as well, but less than the moon
    and sun.
They, too, have an order, to reflect their light, and
    we say, "well done."

The purpose of the clouds, are shade, temperature,
    and regulation.
The order that has been given to them, also includes
    precipitation.

The sky, I call our heavenly dome, is also known as
    celestial sphere.
The order, that has been given to the sky, lets us
    know the Lord is near.

Our Reasonable Service

God doesn't just want our heart; he wants it all; and
      this was from the very start.
Holy, acceptable to God, our reasonable service,
      disobeying him makes me nervous.

We spend our time in the Word of God, even if
      others seem to think it's odd.
That's our reasonable service these days, all he wants
      is to change our ways.

We ourselves must be a sacrifice, if we desire to one
      day live in paradise.
By his mercy, our bodies are presented, but the
      enemy labeled us as a defendant.

Our worship allows him to take control, as we
      humbly surrender our very soul.
We offer the sacrifice of praise, the fruit of our lips,
      giving thanks today as always.

We give back, through our worship of giving, our
      gratitude, and our living.
Through witnessing, we declare your name,
      reminding all, this is not a game.

By worshiping service, we gather at church, opening
     our heart, for God to search.
We sing, clap, cry, and shout, our reasonable service;
     yes! Without a doubt.

We let our light shine for the world to see, and
     remind them, "It's not all about me."
Our only service is to God alone, through mercy
     and truth, iniquity is atoned.

Return from That Place in Life

There's a return from that place in life that most of us experienced.
If we're honest, this is something that caused us great interference.

Our strength was zapped, from that very spirit, that lives in us.
Our character has been changed, while taking away all of our trust.

Never once thought, something like this could happen to you.
Because we were on top of things, how could we miss this by a few.

This place in our life is somewhere we were driven to.
I prayed, because I fret. I just might not make this one through.

I didn't know which way to go, so confused; life made me feel low.
I wasn't that person I was before, I needed to return, and be restored.

I was painfully pulled from a place that was comfortable for me.
Being forced to change how I see life in situations; I wanted to flee.

How could I respectfully return from this place in my life?
Dreams shattered, trust gone, I realized that was the enemy's device.

We can't always return to a place in our lives where we once used to be.
But by God's grace, he could heal our heart, restore, and set us free.

Things change every day, but it's God who helps us change the way.

Rejection

My Lord Jesus Christ was rejected on earth, as is; still today.
He was born in a manger, where baby Jesus would lay.

He didn't come in fancy, or stay at the nearest inn.
He is Savior of the world, born without an ounce of sin.

Rejection is something he is all so familiar about.
When we go through rejection, we need not scream or shout.

Being shun, does not make you feel good at all.
In fact, it appears that you're in between a rock and a hard ball.

It's hard when you're rejected by your family and dear friends.
Then the members, smile, and greet you, while they, too, pretend.

Rejection is not nice, and it hurts to the very heart.
What comes around goes around and could tear you apart.

Being ignored, is simply another form of pushing you away.
For it goes hand in hand with rejection, as some would say.

While we're living on earth, please let us remember this day.
Rejection is a choice, we could choose, "to not be this way."

Signs of the End-Time

In the last days, people will be arrogant, and without self-control.
Disobedient to parents, while slanderous words unfold.
Lovers of self, money, and pleasure, rather than lovers of God.
This is found in 2 Timothy 3 for those who think this is odd.
This is just the beginning, of what's in store for us to come.
Heartlessness and envy have been a rapid norm for some.
The scriptures are sure, and have proven to be true.
Mathew 24:7 reveals what faith believers knew.
Nation rising against nation and kingdom against kingdom.
These end-time signs are noticeable and not just for some.
Famines and earthquakes are in various places.
This has proven to be true, as you study the numerous cases.
Signs of the end-time are here and alive today.
Birth pains, the Word calls it, "Jesus is on his way."
If we remain true, God will help us to make it through.

Speak to My Heart

Speak to my heart, Lord, so that I can hear what
you want to say.
I'm waiting, so that I can give you an answer, and
not delay.

You came to me, in that soft, still voice, the only
one, with a pure choice.
I love to hear you, as you take control of my soul,
and whisper, things untold.

I feel your spirit late in the night, as you confirm;
things will be alright.
Speak to my heart, Lord, for I long to hear, your
presence will forever be near.

I take daily walks, while I shout out your name, you
alone will I proclaim.
I love you so much, my heart leaps with joy, it is
you, whom I employ.

Your words are truth, for you dare not lie, if only we
could satisfy.
You are supreme, only you alone, for you preside,
up on your throne.

Speak to my heart, Lord, so I'll know you're near, to
    chase away all my fears.
When I'm burdened, Lord, and see no way out, you
    direct me to another route.

When I'm sad, and have lost my way, you tell me,
    "Tomorrow is another day."
During death, when I'm in sorrow, you show me
    you who I should follow.

When I can't confide in a friend, it is in you whom
    I depend.
Speak to my heart, Lord, and don't ever let go,
    you're the only one that I owe.

Thank You, Lord

Thank you, Lord, for all you've done for me.
Thank you, Lord, for how you've set me free.

Thank you, Lord, for my life health and my strength.
Thank you, Lord, for allowing me longevity and length.

Thank you, Lord, for being my protector and friend.
Thank you, Lord, for your mercy endures until the end.

Thank you, Lord, for my mom and my dad.
Thank you, Lord, for the good and the bad.

Thank you, Lord, for when I was lost.
Thank you, Lord, for you avoided all cost.

Thank you, Lord, for saving my soul.
Thank you, Lord, for making me whole.

Thank you, Lord, for the thick and the thin.
Thank you, Lord, for forgiving my sin.

Thank you, Lord, for I know one day.
Thank you, Lord, for you're on your way.

Thank you, Lord, for all that you've done.
Thank you, Lord, for your one and only Son.

Teenage Brains

Teenage brains don't operate in the way that grown-ups do.
They can't see the danger in certain situations, in fact, only a few.

They have yet to experience the things we've dealt with in life.
Their dealing with a lot more growing, and a bit of less strife.

They're hard to reach, and this is some of the reasons why.
We refuse to be truthful and open while we lift ourselves in pride.

Hoping they'll read "perfect and role model" as they look at us.
What they see is "dishonest and misleading and a lot of other stuff."

They know things about us, things we thought they never knew.
Because Sue, your brother's wife, shared more conversations than a few.

Let them know about our story, and how imperfect we really are.
Then tell them of how God has brought us along, thus this far.

They see the faults that we have, as they have their own too.
As they began to see that the Father will also help them through.

Share with them, some of our mistakes, and faults we've had.
And maybe, they'll confide in us the things they've encountered in
    the past.

Be truthful to these teenage brains, that we cherish all so dear.
Then maybe they'll confide in us, their struggles and deep fears.

The Blessing of a Child

Children are a blessing, and part of God's creative
    plan.
Through guidance, and discipline, he's placed them
    in a loving hand.

The giggly eyes, and beautiful smile, God alone
    blessed my child.
Through sick or sadness, and even death, he con-
    trols our very breath.

These innocent souls, they look to us, so why do we
    defile their very trust.
We are to love, teach, and bring them up in a way
    so that they won't stray.

Children are a blessing from the Lord, not to be
    thrown away when bored.
They're our future, and hope, our desire is to keep
    them clean, from dope.

We live an honest life around them so that their
    plan would be.
A fair hand, by setting aside, all of our bad habits
    for them to see.

Bring them up in the way of love, by revealing the
    Father from above.
We show them the opposite of hate, which may
    determine their very fate.

By teaching about discrimination, I extend my
    hands to this invitation.
It's called a learned and taught behavior; this is
    frowned on, by my Savior.

Red, yellow, black, or white—makes all of us pre-
    cious in God's sight.
A rainbow of colors, made beautifully, prepared for
    man to be set free.

Thanksgiving

Lord, I am thankful; and I thank you for all you
      have done for me.
Every day is a day of Thanksgiving, as we should
      honor the Lord Almighty.

As we sit around the house, with our dear family
      and friends.
We should all, give thanks unto God, for the time
      he allows us to spend.

Thanksgiving is the expression of gratitude, for all
      that God has blessed us with.
For some, it's too late, they've passed on, like our
      dear friend Mr. Smith.

Being thankful is about seeing another day, that
      we've never seen before.
Or enjoying a meal around the table, with all kinds
      of food, oh, how I adore.

We should also be thankful, for our parents, for they
      have sacrificed for us.
No one's perfect, we, too, have a pass, look in our
      closet, may cause a bit of a fuss.

Some don't have what we've been blessed with, a
      roof covering over our head.
Doesn't mean, they're deemed less, because unfortu-
      nately they don't have a bed.

Blessings come in all sorts of forms, you may have a
	big home, but can't enjoy it.
Through sickness, sadness, death, or even the fact
	that a loved one has split.

Life itself is thanksgiving, because not a day of fresh
	air was promised to us.
God, in his infallible wisdom, has the power to
	allow, and for that we must trust.

Be thankful for the love, that he allowed us to share
	between one another.
And give, as we should, to help our neighbors, our
	sisters, and dear brothers.

The Invisible Me

So often I've become invisible, where no one is able to see.
The identity of the real person, God has placed inside of me.

Who could see me when I'm at work, only those with a hateful smirk?
When I'm shopping, and in the stores, setting aside my daily chores.

Through worship and praise, while in my church.
Invisible shows me, on how well; the enemy lurks.

I could also be invisible in my home, kids of age, so, I'm left alone.
It's not all bad to be invisible, where no one could actually see.

How do I feel, in this life that's so real, is this really a big deal?
How do I feel, they want to know, because Jesus is in charge of this show?

While in my invisibility, what all have I learned.
The ability to sit quietly, while my spirit discerns.

There're perks in being invisible, where no one is able to see.
Your focus is placed on spiritual things, that could one day set you free.

The Love of Money

For the love of money, is the root of all evil.
This is what happens, when our heart is set on
    retrievals.

We brought nothing into this world, and can't take
    anything out.
Money in and of itself, is not evil or good; and that
    is without a doubt.

It is only, what we allow to happen, when it is in
    our hand.
That is why, we should be following, God's amazing
    plan.

There are people, whose only desire in life "is to be
    rich."
After that, they would turn around and throw fam-
    ily, into a ditch.

People have killed loved ones, just to make it big,
    "sold children for a gig."
Money is not relevantly evil, but the love of money
    can make you a weasel.

You turn your back on friends you know, because
    the dollar status told you so.
I understand, about being cautious, but the atti-
    tudes, make me nauseous.

You stop giving to those whose status is less fortu-
    nate from you.
Because of your thinking, you thought, "you've
    already made it through."

The thing about money, we as human beings,
    should always know.
When the Lord calls for us to leave this earth, we
    can't take it to go.

We can't hook it to our casket, or hide it beneath
    our decaying skin.
Because someone, maybe family or friend, will
    remove all, that is within.

So, before the love of money turns your cheery heart
    into stone.
Think of how it would feel, when you're left in this
    world all alone.

The Tongue

The tongue is a fire, a world of evil among the parts of the body.
We bless God, even the Father; and curse men, which is naughty.

Out of the same mouth come praising and cursing.
Like a stage performance, on time for rehearsing.

All kinds of animals, mankind has been able to tame.
The tongue, restless evil, full of deadly poison, "always to blame."

Bits into the mouths of horses to make them obey us.
Even ships, steered by a very small rudder, but we can't hush.

We keep up confusion, by bad-mouthing everywhere we go.
This should be a reminder, this will bring us down, to a new low.

Even friends have lost faith and trust, that has confided in us.
We've shared secrets with others, and felt it shouldn't be a fuss.

Oh, how we've come a long way, where we refuse to keep envy at bay.
By talking so much, we believe the lies we say, and steer no other way.

We all stumble, we're not perfect, anyone could be at fault.
But we have to learn from our mistakes, and not "if we get caught."

With wisdom, which comes from the heaven, and above.
We pray, by asking our Lord to fill our mouth with blessings of love.

Vengeance Is Mine

"Vengeance is mine," said the Lord, "I will repay!
And by my swift action, there will be no delay.

"I know, there're things in life, that could tear you apart.
You must always believe; you will continually be in my heart.

"I was the one that formed you, from my very own hand.
And made it, where you, could eat from the best of the land.

"All that you've gone through, I've experienced it before.
Nothing, that you come to me about, I will ignore.

"I love you so, dear, but I won't change my word.
Recorded and written, you can't say, I've never heard.

"Vengeance is mine," thus says the Lord, "I will repay!
It's time that my people listen, and began to obey.

"Our actions, deed, consequences, in all that we do.
My word can't be broken for one, and favor you.

"Respect of person, I dare not allow."
Jesus formed the way, and has shown us how.

"Love one another, forgive and let go.
Because, I, the Lord, has instructed you so."

Walking with the Lord

Allow me to walk and talk with you, Lord, for this
    is always my desire.
Your love and comfort you've given me; oh, how I
    wonderfully admire.

You speak to my heart, as I listen to your voice, this
    fills my heart with rejoice.
Father, you are God, and God alone, nothing, or no
    one could ever set the tone.

You're awesome, your majesty, in awe, there's no
    greater power, not even the law.
You, Lord, you were born in a manger, being glori-
    fied by a host full of angels.

Oh, how you sit on the throne, you being God has
    the power to atone.

I love you, Lord, I love you dear, when walking with
    you, I know you're near.
You're there when I'm asleep, shielding and protect-
    ing me from all fear.

You provide food on my table, and clothes on my
     back, with you, there's no lack.
Lord, you're the joy of my life, for you alone rid me
     of all pain and strife.

I sing a song unto you because none other has the
     power to bring me through.
Walking with you, Lord, is the best decision of my
     life, this too keeps me away from strife.

Hoping, and praying, while carrying me through.
Directing and protecting is something you do.

We Stand with You

Our heart goes out to the families, that are going through.
We stand with you by faith and prayer, that's what we do.
When you hurt, we hurt, you are not alone.
God is still Lord, and it is he that sits on the throne.
To our leaders, and first responders, all over this nation.
Jesus Christ, our Lord and Savior, is still in control of this situation.
We walk by faith, and not by sight, believing everything will be alright.

What God Opens, No Man Can Close

God has no respect of person, what's done for me, could be for you.
What he opens, no man can close, what he closes, no man gets through.

He looks at the heart of man, and only through him alone.
Can see the inner man, as well as the silent crying and moan.

He dispatches his angels, while broken throughout the night.
And wakes us up, bright and early with a rainbow of his light.

No man can close what he's opened, for you and for me.
It would take not even a lifetime for mankind to see.

His glory, and splendor, nothing could ever come close.
Not even a false god, that some would consider most.

His authority, deems him to sit high, and look down low.
Only through him, who decides, whether he allows it to be so.

He allowed the ocean, their boundary, but to come so far.
Gave wisdom to man, and instructions on how to build a car.

Allowed the sun to shine, and the moon, sets at night.
Then repeat the next morning, a fresh ray of light.

What God opens, no man can close.
We don't understand why, but only he knows.

Were You There?

Were you there, when they crucified my Lord and Savior?
He gave his life, in spite of our out-of-control behavior.

He was beaten, and bruised with no recognition at all.
Because of our sins, it was he who willingly took the fall.

Where you there, when they crucified my Lord on the cross?
Through his death, it was he alone that paid the cost.

How grateful we should be; because of his death, we are made free.
He allows us to come boldly, before his heavenly throne.

He offers us the assurance that he will never leave us alone.

After three days, he rose, and is coming back again.
Where he prepared a home for those who has no sin.

Confess with your mouth, and believe in your heart.
Jesus will hear you, forgive you, and give you a fresh start.

As we humble ourselves before you, dear Lord.
We sincerely ask your forgiveness, and mercy across the board.

What You Allow Is What You Get

What you allow, and settle for in your life, is what
    you get.
Allow that husband, or boyfriend, to treat you bad;
    even when he's unfit.

You've turned your back, didn't say a word, because
    you don't want to offend.
Little do you know, or even, aware, your relation-
    ship with him, is close to an end.

What you allow someone to do, or say to you, is
    truly what you will get.
Sometimes, you have to walk away, instead of allow-
    ing yourself to be hit.

Hold your head high, demand respect, if you don't,
    there'll be an effect.
On your child, your family, and even your friend,
    it's up to you, not to bend.

You smell the fragrance, that's on his clothes, while
    acting like you have no nose.
What you allow, is what you get, he's breaking you
    down bit by bit.

Sometimes, it's good to walk away, which could
        determine, you seeing another day.
Scream, cry, fall down if you must, but don't allow
        someone to steal your trust.

Life's too short, one day at a time, it'll soon pass,
        and your fears will be gone.
You give him your heart, he takes your mind, breaks
        your spirit, and leaves you behind.

Is this what you want your life to be, ten years later,
        thinking why you didn't flee.
What you allow, is what you get, sometimes, the
        best option is for you to split.

Why Me, Lord

I once asked the Lord, "Why me, Father, who am I?"
At that time, I didn't get an answer, nor understood
    why.

I was called, to take a leap of faith, to do something
    you prepared me to do.
I didn't expect that, I became fearful, and ques-
    tioned God, what he knew.

The word declares, that God has no respect of per-
    sons nor partiality.
Whom he decides to choose to do whatever he
    desires, is his, in reality.

He did reply, by saying, why not me, but; who am
    I? Chosen favorably.
My heart melted, because he recognized me, nudg-
    ing me forward, patiently.

I stopped asking, "Lord, why me?" I could be what-
    ever his desire is for me.
As long as, he's with me, shining light through my
    eyes, so I could see.

I'm just a vessel, waiting and willing, allowed to be
    used, for my Savior.
Whatever he does, he and him alone, highly above
    all, awesomely favored.

Who am I? I am a child of the Lord, the love of my
    life, for the world to know.
For I'm not ashamed, and he's not of me, and I
    know, because he told me so.

So, instead of asking him why, I'm trying to learn
    how to trust.
In order for us to please him, the word tells us, it's a
    must.

Words Matter

Words matter; you could use words to build up, or
　　to tear down.
It could put a beautiful smile on your face, or turn
　　it into a frown.

Words could set the tone, for your future, or cause,
　　a spiraling down.
Some determine whether they would live, or turn
　　their life around.

When the love of your life tells you, their love will
　　never fade away.
Then five months later, they're with another person,
　　what are we to say.

Words matter, especially to children, and those that
　　are in their teens.
Words you speak over their life, changes their atti-
　　tude and how they're seen.

Words matter, when you're asked to keep a secret,
　　and you don't.
Your trust and confidence in that person, you really;
　　just do not want.

It's better not to make a vow, than to make one and
    break one.
When it comes to God, our words to him, should
    not be made fun.

Words matter, make a promise to the judge, and
    don't fulfill your deed.
See what they do, it could cause your whole family
    to be in need.

Words matter, lie to the IRS, you're in danger of not
    having a place to live.
Be careful to think before we speak, and be humble
    enough to forgive.

Your word is your bond, when spoken falsely, you
    could cause great harm.
This shows great integrity of oneself; and our spirit
    wouldn't be so alarmed.

Will You Be Ready?

This is just the beginning, call it what you want, but
    prophecy will be fulfilled.
Death and sorrow are everywhere, it seems like this
    nation is going downhill.
Jesus gives us all a choice; the time is now; will you
    listen to his voice?
None of us living are exempt; the devil, our adver-
    sary, that's his main attempt.
John 10:10 says, "The thief cometh not, but for to
    steal, and kill, and to destroy."
But Jesus comes that we may have life; more abun-
    dantly, now, that brings us joy.
It will get worse, Matthew 24:7 tells us, pull up the
    scripture, read it, if you must.
We still have hope, which lies in our Lord, so if we
    perish, we'll still be onboard.
Trust in the Lord, with all your heart, and lean not
    on thine own understanding.
Acknowledge him in all thy ways, it is he, that will
    direct our path these last and evil days.

Wrong Voice in My Head

Whose voice are you listening to, while desperately
striving to make your way through?
The pain of depression is so hard to let go, especially
when the enemy has burdened you so.
He talks to you in your lowest state, hoping that
you would make the ultimate mistake.
To take your life is what he desires, it's not ours to
take, the devil is a liar.
God won't put no more on us to bear, but the
enemy, Satan, he just doesn't care.
We know that mental illness is a sickness, and that
many of our churches, refuse to touch.
But for our Christian family, let's be on the front
line, and not hold our head down, as such.
People are dying through taking their life, being
silent through education is an unbearable fight.
We watch our families, struggle with dope, and turn
our head, while whispering, "No hope!"
Whose voice are we going to listen to? I'll tell you!
It's the one who says, "I love you."
Only God could heal the brokenhearted, life
through him can help you get started.
He's the only one that can heal our pain, close the
void, that's why, he came.
Addiction, mental illness, and depression have to go,
no strength of mine, but because God says so.
As we listen to the wrong voice in our head, make
sure you tell the enemy, Satan, God is not dead.
For he's still alive and he lives in me, and that's why,
I humbly bow my head and bend my knee.

Your Last Words

If you could take back your last words, what would you simply say?
Once words are released, you can never take what's spoken away.
Before someone dies, and harsh words are the last thing they hear.
Spoken hurt words to them, could haunt you with great fear.
My friends, words are so strong, it could pierce our very heart.
Which has often been known to tear entire families apart.
The tongue could never be tamed, for we know this from the Word.
So, we ask God to heal our heart from the things we've already heard.
It's time for us to think before we allow our words to be spoken.
Then we wouldn't have to wonder why our relationships are so broken.
We all have, a bit of the twist of the tongue, which is hurtful, at times.
For we are not perfect, and that's not, the ultimate crime.
Victim shaming, should never be done, to insult the ones we know.
And even if we've never met, it still, shouldn't be as so.
Life's too short to play around, we should have known a long time ago.
We let words that we speak be uplifting, positive, and seasoned as so.

Your Plan for Me

Being retired from my job, was your ultimate, plan for me.
The preparations, I've gone through, only you allowed it, to be.

You've kept me there, while you prepared me, through growth.
While assuring me, of your love, and humbling oath.

You've groomed me, Lord, when I was sixteen years old.
To have an ear to hear, and write, what I was told.

Those thirty-nine years, couldn't see my life heading this way.
You led your dear sis Hill and others in Christ, to boldly say.

It's time to publish, what God has revealed to you.
Not about me, for he allowed, this breakthrough.

I've worked for you, Lord, the minute I said yes.
At times, I felt that my life had become a huge mess.

I didn't understand, the journey, I was called to do.
Frustrated in certain situations, but, only, you knew.

The ride was not easy, but it was worth it all.
To humble myself, and obey the voice of your call.

You're real in my life, as I openly declare.
The one, true living God, who always cared.

Your Amazing Love

Where would I be, Lord, without your precious love?
For you alone has the power to redeem us from above.

Your amazing blood that you shed and died for me.
Father, it's the only reason that I have been made free.

I see your grace and mercy, God, through all of this confusion.
But Satan, our adversary, wants us to believe this is simply an illusion.

I don't know or even understand your plan concerning all of this.
So, I believe by the prayers, and petition, you won't dismiss.

A lot of people are dying, and some won't recover from this pain.
But as a believer, if we die in Christ, it's not a loss but rather gain.

For your Word reveals it's appointed unto men once to die.
Then judgment follows immediately, so now is the time to draw nigh.

Our God is a good God with such an amazing love.
But time runs out, repent; and be delivered from up above.

To God be the glory

My Parents

God has given us two beautiful and wonderful parents.
Who opened their home, and heart; oh, how transparent?

They brought us up, in the Word of God, and helped us to grow.
It has not, been easy for them, nine children; God made it so.

Through the struggles of life, raising us, along the way.
We watched our parents, bend hand and knees, to pray.

They told us, Jesus is the answer, in everything we go through.
But, being a child, growing up in life, we definitely, had no clue.

We watched our parents, along the years, broken, and in pain.
You wonder, "Lord, why go through, and what are we to gain?"

These two wonderful parents, who were given, to us all.
I'm thankful for the vision, and the hearing of your call.

What would have happened, if we didn't have both of you.
His plan was to prosper, not harm, in all you've gone through.

Now, we see the fruits of their labor, from the storm and rain.
This was all due, in preparation, knowing, it was not in vain.

About the Author

Jackie Moody is a devout Christian. She is a dedicated wife and mother to her husband, Steve, and two daughters, Shani and Crystal, and stepdaughter, Tasha.

At the age of sixteen, Jackie entered a competition entitled Teen Talent, which was sponsored by her church, which gave teenagers the opportunity to display their gifts and talents.

She decided to give poetry writing a try. As she prepared to write, God not only divinely inspired her to write and publish her first book called *Revelation of the Time*, he also literally gave her the words to write her second book, *Unveiled by Truth: The Word of God.*

God continues to use her to write poems to this day, and she continues to allow him to do so as she writes with love, sincerity, and passion.